PYTHON GAME DEVELOPER'S ODYSSEY

A COMPREHENSIVE GUIDE FROM FUNDAMENTALS TO MASTERING ADVANCED TECHNIQUES, DESIGN PRINCIPLES, AND PUBLISHING STRATEGIES

Contents

8

Explain

The universe of gaming is a fascinating space that has grown conclusively all through the long haul. With the presence of advancement, the degree and multifaceted design of games have expanded, offering striking experiences that transcend basic entertainment. Because of its comprehensibility, usability, and broad assortment of libraries like Pygame, Python, a flexible and strong programming language, has arisen as a well known decision for game turn of events.

This acquaintance opens the entryway with the captivating universe of Python game turn of events, where tomfoolery and development meet rationale and imagination. We'll learn about game plan basics, Python's game-making capabilities, and how to revitalize virtual universes as we embark on this journey.

The Charm of Game New development

Games have always been a comprehensive language, transcending social and phonetic cutoff points. From model tabletop games to refined virtual circumstances, the hankering for shrewd and attracting experiences has been a consistent in humankind's arrangement of encounters. The creation of universes in which players can escape, learn, and interact is the result of game turn of events, which is both a science and a craft.

The rise of Python in the game development industry is evidence of the language's adaptability and accessibility. Python provides a friendly and instinctive environment for communicating

11

your game ideas, regardless of whether you are a coding novice or a meticulous designer. This guide will tell us the best way to utilize Python to its fullest potential, digging into the different phases of game turn of events, from clear amusements of works of art to complicated, unique manifestations.

The Rise of Python in Game Development Python's rise from a widely used pre-planning language to a prominent player in game development is fantastic. While Python isn't regularly associated with world class execution plans and raised reenactments, its comfort and expansive libraries have attracted engineers searching for a congruity among straightforwardness and helpfulness.

Pygame, a lot of Python modules planned for game development, plays had a critical effect in's first experience with the gaming scene. With Pygame, designers can saddle the power of Python to make 2D games no perspiration, making game improvement open to a greater group.

Setting the Stage: Your Headway Environment

Before we dive into the charming space of game development, setting up a supportive improvement climate is essential. Having the right instruments and an efficient work area is vital for a smooth and useful improvement process, whether or not you are a carefully prepared engineer or a beginner.

In this associate, we'll walk you through the method for setting up your Python environment, presenting significant libraries, and planning your workspace. From picking the right code boss to understanding variation control, each piece of your improvement environment will be meticulously investigated to ensure a steady journey through the universe of Python game development.

Investigating the Associate

This guide is coordinated to take you on an intensive trip through various pieces of Python game new development. We'll start with the essentials, familiarizing you with principal Python thoughts and guiding you through the foundation of Pygame. As we progress, we'll examine excellent game changes, delineations and development, shrewd describing, GUI games with Tkinter, and even dive into the space of multiplayer games.

The aid is designed to be interactive, with useful models, coding activities, and projects provided in each section to enhance your learning. These pages will furnish you with an abundance of data whether you are keen on learning progressed game improvement methods, redoing immortal works of art, or making your own game without any preparation.

Utilizing Game Advancement to Release Imagination Game improvement is something other than composing code; it's connected to delivering creative mind and changing contemplations into instinctive experiences. Through this helper, you'll not simply gotten comfortable with the specific pieces of Python game development yet what's more track down how to embed your endeavors with character, story, and an exceptional character.

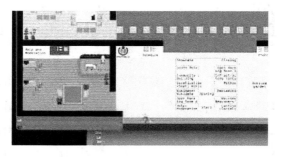

You will acquire bits of knowledge that go past lines of code as we explore the scene of game plan standards, dive into the intricacies of UI (UI) plan, and fathom the subtleties of player experience (PX) plan. You'll sort out some way to captivate players, make significant gaming minutes, and workmanship experiences that leave a persevering through impact.

Game improvement is a one-of-a-kind field that is constantly evolving in response to new developments and shifting player expectations. As you set out on this trip, desire to encounter troubles, tackle complex issues, and, specifically, experience constant improvement as a designer.

In the areas that follow, we'll not simply helper you through the particular pieces of game development yet furthermore ask you to embrace challenges as any entryways for learning and improvement. You'll develop the adaptability and adaptability necessary for success in the ever-evolving scene of game turn of events by investigating common issues, improving game execution, and participating in game challenges.

The Far ahead

As we investigate through Python game development, recall that this guide is an early phase for your trip. The knowledge and skills you acquire here will serve as a foundation for investigating more advanced topics and pushing the boundaries of your imagination.

Whether you attempt to cultivate games skillfully, add to the open-source gaming neighborhood, essentially share during the time spent making instinctive experiences, this guide is custom fitted to connect with you. Accordingly, could we leave on this experience together, where coding meets imaginativeness, and the possible results are essentially pretty much as huge as your innovative brain. Get ready to deliver the capacity of Python in the entrancing universe of game new development!

1.1 An Overview of Python Games

The Landscape of Python Game Development Before delving into the specifics of Python game development, it is essential to comprehend the broader landscape and Python's place in this ever-evolving field. Games, going from exemplary control center titles to current portable applications, are based on different innovations, each filling a particular need. Python, with its effortlessness and flexibility, has arisen as a convincing decision for an assortment of game improvement situations.

In this part, we'll investigate the kinds of games Python succeeds at making, look at the qualities and constraints of the language for game turn of events, and feature key systems and libraries that make Python an important apparatus in a game engineer's weapons store.

Sorts of Python Games

2D Games: Python, especially with the Pygame library, is appropriate for creating 2D games. These games range from straightforward side-looking over experiences to complex riddle tackling difficulties.

Text-based Games: Because it is easy to read, Python is a great choice for text-based games where the story and making decisions are more important than graphics.

Instructive Games: Python is every now and again utilized in the improvement of instructive games, giving an intelligent and connecting with stage for picking up programming ideas.

Qualities and Limits

Simplicity of Learning: Python's punctuation is clear and direct, making it open to amateurs. This simplicity of learning speeds up the game improvement process, permitting designers to zero in on imagination.

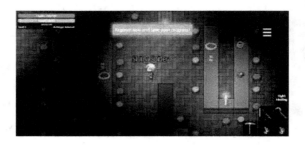

Community Assistance: The Python people group is energetic and strong. A plenty of assets, instructional exercises, and gatherings are accessible for game designers to look for help, share information, and team up.

Taking into account performance: While Python isn't known for elite execution calculations, for the majority game sorts, particularly those not intensely dependent on constant delivering, its exhibition is frequently adequate. Nonetheless, in cases requiring complex recreations or many-sided designs, different dialects might be liked.

Key Systems and Libraries

Pygame: A well known cross-stage set of Python modules intended for game turn of events, giving capabilities to taking care of designs, sound, and client input.

Ren'Py: Explicitly custom-made for visual books and intelligent narrating, Ren'Py improves on the making of account driven games.

Arcade: A cutting edge Python structure for building 2D games, offering a spotless and straightforward Programming interface while being profoundly extensible.

Python's Part in the Gaming Environment

Python's part in the gaming environment stretches out past being a language for game turn of events. It is additionally utilized in different limits all through the gaming business. From robotization in game testing to prearranging for server-side rationale, Python's adaptability makes it a significant apparatus for game designers, analyzers, and managers the same.

As we continue through this aide, we'll unwind the layers of Python's commitment to the gaming scene, investigating how it empowers designers to rejuvenate their thoughts and partake in the consistently developing scene of intuitive diversion.

1.2 Setting Up Your Improvement Climate

Making a Helpful Work area

Before we leave on our Python game improvement venture, laying out an efficient and productive advancement climate is essential. A painstakingly designed work area upgrades efficiency as well as guarantees a smooth progress among learning and making.

Visual Studio Code's IDE or Code Editor: A lightweight, extensible code supervisor with powerful Python support and a rich environment of expansions.

PyCharm: a powerful Python IDE with advanced tools for debugging and code analysis, as well as support for integrated testing.

Introducing Python and Overseeing Conditions

Introducing Python: Bit by bit manual for introducing Python on your framework, guaranteeing similarity with the game improvement libraries and systems canvassed in this aide.

Virtual Conditions: An introduction to the use of virtual environments to separate project dependencies and keep the development environment clean and manageable.

Variant Control and Joint effort

Git: Outline of variant control with Git, fundamental for following changes, working together with others, and guaranteeing project steadiness.

GitHub or GitLab: Providing a platform for sharing your game projects with the community, hosting platforms for version

control repositories, and encouraging collaboration
Organizing Code for Your Project Structure: Best practices for organizing your game activities to upgrade comprehensibility, practicality, and coordinated effort.
Resources and Assets: Overseeing game resources, including pictures, sounds, and different assets, in an organized way.

Testing Your Arrangement
Hi World in Pygame: A straightforward "Hi World" model

utilizing Pygame to confirm that your improvement climate is designed accurately.

Running a Test Venture: Making and running a fundamental Python content to guarantee that your code proofreader or IDE is appropriately set up.

As we continue through this aide, a very much designed improvement climate will be the establishment for releasing the maximum capacity of Python in game turn of events. Thus, we should focus in and guarantee that our work area is prepared for the thrilling excursion ahead!

2. Beginning with Fundamental Ideas

2.1 Factors and Information Types

Grasping Factors

What are Factors: Prologue to factors as holders for putting away information. explanation of the significance of variables in game and programming development.

Variable Naming Shows: Best practices for naming factors to improve code intelligibility and practicality.

Information Types in Python: Outline of essential information types like whole numbers, floats, strings, and booleans.

Working with Factors

Variable Task: how to update and assign values to variables throughout the program.

Type Transformation: Investigating strategies to change over between various information types when fundamental.

Changeless versus Alterable Sorts: Understanding the qualification between types that can be changed set up (variable) and those that can't (permanent).

Practice Activities

Basic Estimations: Composing Python scripts for fundamental number-crunching activities to build up factor utilization.

String Control: Making contents to control strings, showing the adaptability of string factors.

2.2 Control Stream (if proclamations, circles)

Contingent Articulations (if, elif, else)

Prologue to if Proclamations: Involving restrictive explanations to settle on choices in code in light of specific circumstances.

elif and else Conditions: Extending restrictive explanations to deal with different cases.

Settled if Proclamations: Understanding the idea of settling if articulations for more complicated navigation.

Circles (for and keeping in mind that)

Prologue to Circles: Outline of for and keeping in mind that circles as iterative designs in Python.

Circle Control Articulations (break, proceed): Understanding how to modify circle conduct utilizing break and proceed with proclamations.

Settled Circles: Using settled circles for dealing with complex information or performing rehashed undertakings.

Practice Activities

Odd/Much Number Checker: Composing a content that decides if a given number is odd or in any event, utilizing contingent explanations.

Commencement Clock: Carrying out a commencement clock utilizing some time circle to rehearse circle structures.

2.3 Capabilities and Modules

Capabilities in Python

Characterizing Capabilities: Making capabilities to embody blocks of code for reusability.

Capability Boundaries and Bring Values back: Understanding how to pass boundaries to capabilities and get bring values back.

Extent of Factors: Talking about neighborhood and worldwide degree, stressing the significance of variable extension in capabilities.

Modules in Python: An Overview of Modules: Outline of modules as a method for coordinating code into isolated records.

Making and Bringing in Modules: Composing your own modules and bringing them into different contents.

Standard Library Modules: Investigating regularly utilized modules from the Python Standard Library.

Practice Activities

Capability Number cruncher: Building a number cruncher with essential math tasks utilizing capabilities.

Module Investigation: Making a straightforward module containing reusable capabilities and bringing it into a primary content.

You will acquire a solid understanding of Python's syntax

and structure as we delve into these fundamental concepts, preparing you for more complex game development topics. The capacity to work with factors, control stream, capabilities, and modules shapes the foundation of compelling Python programming and will enable you as you progress through the resulting segments of this aide.

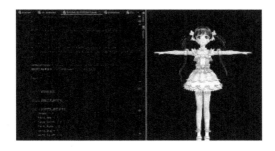

3. Prologue to Pygame
3.1 Introducing Pygame
What is Pygame?

Outline of Pygame: Prologue to Pygame as a bunch of Python modules intended for game turn of events.

Highlights and Capacities: Featuring key elements, like taking care of designs, sound, and client input, that settle on Pygame a famous decision for 2D game turn of events.

Introducing Pygame

Utilizing pip: Bit by bit guide on introducing Pygame utilizing the Python bundle administrator, pip.

Checking Establishment: Running a basic Pygame content to affirm that the library is accurately introduced.

3.2 Making a Basic Pygame Window

Setting Up Your Pygame Venture

Making a Venture Envelope: Sorting out your game improvement projects with devoted envelopes.

Instating Pygame: Composing the standard code to introduce Pygame and set up the super game circle.

Pygame Nuts and bolts

The Pygame Show: utilizing the display module of Pygame to create a window for your game.

Dealing with Occasions: Prologue to occasion dealing with to catch client input and answer occasions like key presses and mouse clicks.

Refreshing the Showcase: Figuring out the idea of refreshing the presentation inside the game circle.

Practice Venture: Hello Pygame, Building a Basic Game Window: Building an essential Pygame window to get involved insight with Pygame's showcase capacities.

How to Handle Quit Events: Executing code to close the game window when the client taps the nearby button.

Adding Color to the Background: Tweaking the presence of the game window by setting a foundation tone.

3.3 Pygame Designs and Movement

Pygame Surfaces and Drawing

Pygame Surfaces: Drawing graphics in Pygame starts with comprehending surfaces.

Drawing Shapes: investigating techniques for drawing fundamental shapes, lines, and rectangles on Pygame surfaces.

Stacking and Showing Pictures: Integrating pictures into your

Pygame task to improve visual components.

Liveliness in Pygame

Outline Rate and Time: Managing your game's frame rate for smooth animation.

Vitalizing Sprites: Making energized characters or items by showing a grouping of pictures.

Symbol Sheets: Using sprite sheets to deal with various casings of movement proficiently.

Project for Practice: Enlivened Character

Making a Person Class: Planning a Python class to address an energized character in your game.

Executing Liveliness: Coordinating sprite sheets and quickening your personality inside the Pygame window.

Client Contribution for Movement: allowing the character's movement and animation to be controlled by user input.

3.4 Understanding Pygame

Events and Handling User-Inputted Events: recognizing the various kinds of user-generated events.

Console Info: controlling game elements by recording key presses and releases.

Mic input: Dealing with mouse occasions for intuitive ongoing interaction.

Answering Client Info

Refreshing Game State: Adjusting the game state in view of client input.

Carrying out Player Controls: assigning specific actions to mouse clicks or key presses.

Mouse Position and Snap Discovery: Integrating the mouse position for exact association.

Practice Undertaking: Player-controlled Game Item

Making a Player Class: Planning a class to address a game item constrained by the player.

Executing Player Controls: Using console contribution to move the player-controlled object inside the game window.

Intelligent Components: Integrating intuitive components that answer client input.

As you dive into the domain of Pygame, you'll not just addition a strong groundwork in making a game window yet in addition investigate the thrilling prospects of designs, movement, and client input. These abilities will act as the structure blocks for growing more mind boggling and drawing in games in the ensuing segments of this aide.

4. Exemplary Games Changes
4.1 Snake Game

- Understanding the Snake Game
- Game Guidelines and Mechanics: Outline of the exemplary Snake game's guidelines and how the game advances.
- Game Targets: Characterizing the essential goals of the Snake game and the circumstances for winning or losing.
- Executing the Snake Game in Python
- Making the Game Window: Making the Pygame window into the game's canvas.
- Snake Development: Carrying out the rationale for the snake's development in light of client input.
- Game Over: Laying out the really game circle to deal with constant ongoing interaction.

- Game Mechanics and Elements
- Developing the Snake: designing the mechanism by which the snake grows when it eats.
- Impact Location: Taking care of crashes between the snake, walls, and itself.
- Scorekeeping: Carrying out a scoring framework to follow the player's advancement.
- Project for Practice: Building the Snake Class: Snake Game Creating a Python class to encapsulate the snake's behavior and represent it.
- Making Food Items: establishing a class for the items that the snake will consume as food.
- Game Over Screen: Executing a game over screen with the choice to restart the game.

4.2 Tetris Clone

- Figuring out Tetris
- Tetris Interactivity: Investigating the standards and mechanics of the exemplary Tetris game.
- Shapes and Turn: Distinguishing the various Tetris shapes and carrying out turn usefulness.
- Executing a Tetris Clone in Python
- Making the Game Lattice: establishing the grid on which the Tetris pieces will fall.
- Block Development: Executing the rationale for moving Tetris obstructs left, right, and descending.
- Game Circle for Tetris: Laying out a consistent game circle to deal with falling blocks and client input.
- Tetris Elements and Difficulties

- Clearing Lines: Planning the component for clearing finished lines and scoring focuses.
- Arbitrary Block Age: generating random Tetris blocks that can be controlled by the player.
- Game Over Conditions: Carrying out conditions for finishing the game in view of block stacking.
- Project for Practice: Block Class: Tetris Clone Tetris Making a class to address Tetris obstructs and deal with their way of behaving.
- Scoring Framework: Carrying out a scoring framework in light of the quantity of lines cleared.
- Game Over Screen: Showing a game over screen with choices to restart or exit.

4.3 Pong Game

- Figuring out Pong

- Pong Interactivity: Outline of the exemplary Pong game's mechanics and goals.
- Paddle Development: defining the paddle movement based on input from users.
- Carrying out a Pong Game in Python
- Setting Up the Game Field: Making the game window and setting up the play region.
- Interaction with Paddle: Executing the rationale for paddle development and crash location.
- Ball Development: Planning the development of the ball and taking care of impacts with oars and walls.
- Pong Elements and Improvements
- Scoring Framework: Executing a scoring component for following player focuses.

- Ball Speed Variety: Presenting varieties in ball speed for added challenge.
- Game Over Conditions: Characterizing conditions for finishing the game in light of player execution.
- Project for Practice: Classes of Pong paddles and balls: Creating Python classes to address the oars and ball in the game.
- Score Show: Showing the ongoing score during interactivity.
- Game Over Screen: implementing a game-ending screen with restart and exit options.

You will not only recreate the nostalgic experience as you embark on the journey of remaking classic games, but you will also gain valuable insights into game mechanics, design, and programming. These tasks will act as a strong starting point for handling further developed game improvement ideas in the ensuing segments of this aide.

5. Illustrations and Movement

5.1 Drawing Shapes and Pictures

Pygame Drawing Essentials

Drawing on the Pygame Surface: Understanding the Pygame Surface as the material for drawing.

Drawing Shapes: Using Pygame capabilities to draw essential shapes like square shapes, circles, and lines.

Variety Portrayal: exploring Pygame's color representation and how to use it to improve graphics.

Picture Taking care of in Pygame

Stacking Pictures: Stacking outer pictures into your Pygame project.

Showing Pictures: Drawing pictures on the Pygame Surface for visual portrayal.

Picture Straightforwardness: Taking care of straightforwardness in pictures for more consistent reconciliation.

Project for Practice: Mathematical Workmanship

Making a Material: Making a geometric art canvas out of a Pygame window.

Drawing Shapes Progressively: Executing client controlled drawing of shapes utilizing mouse input.

Stacking and Showing Pictures: Integrating pictures into the workmanship material.

5.2 Energizing Game Articles

Grasping Activity in Games

Outline based Movement: Presenting the idea of casing based movement in games.

Refreshing Game State: Connecting liveliness to the constant update of the game state.

The Revisited Sprite Sheets: Advancing liveliness with sprite sheets for smoother changes.

Carrying out Liveliness in Pygame

Vitalizing Sprites: Making movements for game items utilizing a grouping of pictures.

Invigorating Development: Integrating liveliness into the development of characters or articles.

Control of frame rates: Changing the casing rate to accomplish the ideal movement speed.

Project for Practice: Energized Character Development

Character Sprite Sheet: making an animated character's sprite sheet.

Vitalizing Person Development: Incorporating the person's development with movements.

Client Contribution for Movement: Permitting client contribution to control both development and livelinesss.

5.3 Dealing with Client Info

Pygame Occasions and Info Dealing with

Grasping Pygame Occasions: recognizing the various kinds of user-generated events.

Console Info: Catching key presses and deliveries for controlling game components.

Mic input: Dealing with mouse occasions for intuitive ongoing interaction.

Answering Client Info

Refreshing Game State: Adjusting the game state in view of client input.

Carrying out Player Controls: assigning specific actions to mouse clicks or key presses.

Mouse Position and Snap Discovery: Integrating the mouse position for exact association.

Project for Practice: Intuitive Designs

Making Intuitive Components: Executing buttons, sliders, or draggable articles.

Mouse Collaboration: incorporating mouse events into interactive element actions.

Dynamic Illustrations Adjustment: dynamically modifying or creating graphics through user input.

As you investigate illustrations and liveliness in this segment, you'll figure out how to revive your games by consolidating outwardly engaging components and dynamic activities. These abilities will altogether upgrade the player experience and set up for further developed game advancement ideas in the accompanying segments of this aide.

6. Intuitive Narrating Games

6.1 Making a Text-Based Experience

Prologue to Intuitive Narrating

What is Intuitive Narrating: Grasping the idea of intuitive narrating in games.

Stretching Stories: Investigating making different story branches in view of player decisions.

Text-Based versus Visual Narrating: Contrasting text-based and visual narrating approaches.

Carrying out a Text-Based Experience in Python

Story Design: defining the interactive story's structure, which includes decision nodes and plot points.

Client Info Taking care of: capturing user feedback for decision-making and story advancement.

Various Endings: creating multiple story endings based on the choices made by players.

Project for Practice: Pick Your Experience

Making a Story Layout: Arranging the account design, decisions, and results.

Executing Story Rationale: Creating Python code to carry out the narrative based on choices made by users.

Client Communication: Showing the story and inciting the client for input.

6.2 Decision based Story Games

Prologue to Decision based Story Games

Intuitive Fiction Games: Understanding the class of decision based story games.

Making Choice Focuses: determining when players make

choices that have an impact on the plot.

Character Formation: Integrating character circular segments and advancement through player decisions.

Python Decision Trees and a Choice-Based Story Game: Imagining and carrying out choice trees to deal with the story stream.

Character Factors: Following person characteristics and connections in view of player decisions.

Detail Following: presenting game statistics that are influenced by player choices.

Project for Practice: Decision based Account

Characterizing Story Ways: Framing different story ways and endings.

Executing Choice Focuses: Creating Python code to handle player choices and alter the narrative.

Envisioning Decisions: Making a UI to show decisions and results.

As you jump into intuitive narrating games, you'll investigate the combination of account and player organization. These undertakings will direct you through making vivid and connecting with encounters where players' choices shape the unfurling story. In the following sections of this guide, you will work toward more complex narrative-driven game development using the skills you learn here.

7. Building a Tic-Tac-Toe Game Using Tkinter for GUI Games

7.1 An Overview of Tkinter

Outline of Tkinter as the standard GUI (Graphical UI) library for Python.

Benefits of Tkinter: Examining the straightforwardness and usability of Tkinter for making graphical connection points.

Tkinter widgets include Understanding normal gadgets like buttons, marks, and passage fields.

Carrying out an Essential GUI with Tkinter

Making a Tkinter Window: Setting up the principal window for the GUI.

Adding Buttons and Marks: Integrating buttons and marks to make an intuitive point of interaction.

Dealing with Occasions: Characterizing capabilities to deal with button clicks and other client associations.

Representation of the Tic-Tac-Toe Game's Logic Game Board: Planning an information construction to address the Spasm Tac-Toe game board.

Player Turns and Checking Cells: Executing rationale for players to alternate and check cells on the board.

Winning Circumstances: Checking for winning circumstances and proclaiming a champ.

Project for Practice: Tic-Tac-Toe Building the GUI with Tkinter: Making the Spasm Tac-Toe game connection point with Tkinter.

Coordinating Game Rationale: Associating the graphical point of interaction with the basic game rationale.

How to Handle Player Input: Permitting players to tap on cells to take their actions.

7.2 Memory Puzzle Game

Memory Puzzle Game Idea

Memory and Focus Games: Understanding the idea of memory-based games.

Layouts based on a grid: discussing the organization of game elements through the use of grids.

Animation of flipping cards: Presenting vitalizing card flips in the memory game.

Executing a Memory Puzzle Game with Tkinter

Making a Framework of Cards: Planning a framework design for the memory puzzle game.

Randomizing Card Positions: Rearranging the cards to guarantee an alternate plan each time.

Card Flipping Component: Carrying out movements for flipping cards and uncovering their appearances.

Memory Game Rationale

Match Matching Rationale: Characterizing the rationale for matching sets of cards.

Game Finish Check: Deciding when the player has effectively paired all matches.

Scoring Framework: Carrying out a scoring framework in light of the quantity of moves made.

Project for Practice: Building the Game Interface: Tkinter Memory Puzzle utilizing Tkinter to design the memory puzzle's graphical user interface.

Incorporating Game Rationale: connecting the game's underlying logic to the graphical elements.

Improving Client Experience: adding features like a reset button and a score display.

As you investigate GUI game improvement with Tkinter, you'll figure out how to make intuitive and outwardly engaging games with a graphical UI. These undertakings won't just acquaint you with Tkinter yet in addition give significant bits of knowledge into building games that clients can appreciate in an all the more outwardly captivating way.

8. Multiplayer Games

8.1 Prologue to Attachments

Essentials of Systems administration

What is Organizing: Understanding the essentials of PC organizing.

Client-Server Model: Investigating the client-server engineering for multiplayer games.

IP and port numbers: Understanding how PCs on an organization speak with one another.

Attachments in Python

What are Attachments: Prologue to attachments as a component for correspondence between gadgets.

Attachment Types: distinguishing between TCP and UDP sockets and their various applications.

The socket Module in Python: Outline of Python's implicit attachment module for attachment programming.

8.2 Structure a Straightforward Multiplayer Game

Game Plan for Multiplayer

Multiplayer Game Ideas: comprehending the difficulties and factors of multiplayer game design.

Client-Server Association: Characterizing how clients and servers impart in a multiplayer climate.

Synchronization of Game States: Guaranteeing that all players have a reliable perspective on the game world.

Server Execution

Setting Up the Game Server: Making a server to oversee associations and game state.

Dealing with Various Clients: Carrying out a server that can deal with numerous client associations simultaneously.

Game Rationale on the Server: putting the game logic in one place on the server to keep things consistent.

Client Execution

Associating with the Server: constructing a client that is capable of connecting to the game server.

Client Info and Activities: Permitting players to send contribution to the server and get refreshes.

Delivering Multiplayer Game State: Showing the game state got from the server.

Project for Practice: Straightforward Multiplayer Game

Planning a Straightforward Game: Framing the guidelines and mechanics of an essential multiplayer game.

Carrying out Server-Client Communication: Fostering the server and client parts for the multiplayer game.

Testing with Numerous Clients: Checking that various clients can associate and play together.

8.3 Internet based Multiplayer Game Contemplations

Versatility and Execution

Server Burden Adjusting: Methods for dispersing player connections across multiple servers.

Upgrading Game State Updates: Limiting how much information sent between the server and clients for productivity.

Reducing latency and lag: Procedures for decreasing inactivity and giving a smoother multiplayer experience.

Security and Confirmation

Player Confirmation: Carrying out secure strategies for confirming player characters.

Information Encryption: Guaranteeing that correspondence among clients and servers is secure.

Hostile to Swindling Measures: Procedures for recognizing and forestalling deceiving in web based games.

Local area and Social Elements

Talk Frameworks: putting chat features into the game for player communication.

Achievements and Leader boards: Acquainting serious and social components with improve player commitment.

Entryway Frameworks: Making spaces for players to sort out and join games.

The complexities of designing and implementing games that connect players from different locations will become clear to you as you explore multiplayer game development.

These undertakings will give an establishment to making further developed multiplayer encounters and furnish you with the information to explore the difficulties of internet gaming.

9. High level Game Improvement Methods

9.1 Game Material science and Recreations

Material science in Game Turn of events

Significance of Material science: Understanding the job of material science in making sensible and vivid games.

Dynamics of a Rigid Body: Recreating the development and communications of unbending bodies in a game world.

Crash Recognition and Goal: Distinguishing crashes between game items and settling them suitably.

Executing Physical science in Python

Material science Motor Incorporation: Investigating well known physical science motors for

Python, like Pygame's implicit physical science.

Custom Physical science Reenactment: Building an essential custom physical science reenactment for straightforward games.

Project for Practice: Physical science based Game

Planning a Physical science based Game: Illustrating the idea and mechanics of a game that vigorously depends on material science.

Executing Material science Rationale: Coordinating material science reenactments into the game for sensible cooperations.

Testing and Tweaking Material science Boundaries: Calibrating the physical science boundaries for ideal interactivity.

9.2 Man-made consciousness in Games

Computer based intelligence in Game Turn of events

Job of computer based intelligence in Games: Understanding how man-made brainpower improves ongoing interaction encounters.

Game man-made intelligence Procedures: Investigating strategies, for example, pathfinding, choice trees, and state machines.

Contrarian AI: Making wise adversaries that challenge players.

Carrying out man-made intelligence in Python

Pathfinding Calculations: Carrying out calculations like A* for effective route of game characters.

Choice Trees and Conduct Trees: Planning dynamic frameworks for game elements.

State Machines: Executing state-based simulated intelligence for overseeing character conduct.

Project for Practice: Man-made intelligence driven Game

Planning the Game Idea: Illustrating a game that intensely depends on computer based intelligence driven characters.

Putting AI Logic into Use: Coordinating computer based intelligence ways of behaving, for example, pathfinding and independent direction.

Adjusting AI Toughness: Changing boundaries to make a difficult yet charming gaming experience.

9.3 Increased Reality (AR) Games

Prologue to Increased Reality

What is AR: Recognizing the significance of augmented reality to game development.

AR Structures and Libraries: Investigating famous AR improvement apparatuses and libraries.

Marker-based versus Markerless AR: Separating between marker-based and markerless AR draws near.

Carrying out AR in Python

AR Game Advancement Apparatuses: Outline of Python libraries and structures for AR improvement.

Marker Following: Executing marker-based AR for perceiving and following markers.

Overlaying Virtual Items: Using augmented reality to embed virtual objects in the real world.

Project for Practice: AR Game

Planning an AR Game Idea: describing a game using augmented reality technology.

Putting AR Features into Use: Coordinating marker following and virtual item situation into the game.

Testing and Streamlining AR Experience: Guaranteeing a smooth and vivid AR gaming experience.

9.4 Game Improvement with AI

AI in Game Turn of events

Utilizations of ML in Games: Investigating regions where AI upgrades game turn of events.

Preparing Models for Interactivity: Utilizing AI to make versatile and responsive game components.

Production of procedural content: Creating game substance utilizing AI calculations.

Carrying out ML in Python

Combination with Game Motors: Associating AI models with well known game motors.

Support Learning: Carrying out support learning for preparing clever game specialists.

Gameplay driven by data: adjusting game dynamics and analyzing player behavior with machine learning.

Project for Practice: ML-driven Game Component

Distinguishing ML Amazing open doors: Distinguishing a game component that can profit from AI.

Preparing ML Models: Planning and preparing AI models for the game.

Incorporating ML into the Game: Executing the prepared models into the game for dynamic ongoing interaction.

As you investigate progressed game advancement methods, you'll acquire bits of knowledge into making refined and state of the art gaming encounters. These undertakings won't just grow your specialized abilities yet additionally acquaint you with arising advancements that assume a critical part in molding the eventual fate of intuitive diversion.

10. Principles of Game Design

10.1 An Understanding of Game Design What Is Game Design?

Meaning of Game Plan: Grasping the complex discipline of game plan.

Components of a Game: Recognizing the fundamental parts that make up a game.

Player Experience: Perceiving the significance of planning for player commitment and delight.

Process of Game Design Conceptualization: Conceptualizing and conceptualizing game thoughts.

Prototyping: Making introductory models to test and emphasize on game mechanics.

Iterative Plan: Embracing an iterative plan process for ceaseless improvement.

10.2 Player Brain science and Inspiration

Player Inspiration

Player Types: Investigating player prime examples and inspirations in gaming.

Player Prizes: comprehending how player motivation is affected by progression and reward systems.

Characteristic versus Extraneous Inspiration: recognizing the differences between motivation from within and outside oneself.

Player Commitment

Stream State: Establishing a climate that encourages a condition of stream for players.

Adjusting Challenge and Expertise: Guaranteeing that game difficulties line up with player expertise levels.

Story Commitment: Consolidating convincing stories to dazzle players.

10.3 Game Mechanics and Elements

Game Mechanics

Meaning of Game Mechanics: Distinguishing the guidelines and frameworks that administer player connections.

The Fundamentals: Figuring out essential activities and ways of behaving in a game.

Developing Ongoing interaction: Taking into account surprising and rising encounters through game mechanics.

Adjusting and Tuning

Game Adjusting: Guaranteeing fair and pleasant ongoing interaction through balance changes.

Pacing: directing the game's tempo and rhythm to maximize player engagement.

Criticism Frameworks: Executing input components to impart data to players.

10.4 UI (UI) and Client Experience (UX) Plan

UI/UX Standards

UI Plan: designing user-friendly and visually appealing interfaces.

Client Experience Plan: Zeroing in on the general insight of players all through the game.

Accessibility: Guaranteeing that the game is open to a different crowd.

Design of the Interaction and Navigation Menu: Creating menus and connection points for simple route.

Control Planning: Planning controls to advance player collaboration.

Consistency: Keeping a steady UI/UX plan all through the game.

10.5 The Importance of Storytelling and Narrative

Design in Video Games: acknowledging the significance of

narrative in shaping player experiences.

Player Organization: Permitting players to impact the unfurling account through their decisions.

World Structure: Making vivid and sound game universes.

Story Components

Character Advancement: Making convincing and appealing characters.

Layout of the Story: creating a narrative arc that is both engaging and well-structured.

Player-Driven Stories: Consolidating player choices to shape the story.

10.6 Strategies for Game Monetization

Monetization Models Free-to-Play (F2P): Offering the game for nothing with discretionary in-game buys.

Pay-to-Play: Requiring a forthright installment for admittance to the game.

Membership Models: Charging players on a common reason for proceeded with access.

In-Game Buys

Microtransactions: Carrying out little exchanges for virtual products or advantages.

Plunder Boxes and Gacha Frameworks: Presenting randomized prizes through virtual thing boxes.

Adjusting Adaptation and Player Experience: ensuring monetization practices that are fair and ethical.

10.7 Playtesting and Client Criticism

Significance of Playtesting

Playtesting Interaction: Including players in the testing stage to assemble criticism.

Iterative Plan: utilizing the feedback from playtests to refine and enhance game elements.

Variety in Playtesters: ensuring a wide range of playtesters with a wide range of perspectives.

Examining Client Criticism

Quantitative Information: evaluating numerical data, such as player statistics and metrics.

Subjective Criticism: Taking into account emotional player input for nuanced experiences.

Adjusting Vision and Input: achieving the right balance between the player's preferences and the designer's vision.

10.8 Moral Contemplations in Game Plan

Dependable Plan

Portrayal: Guaranteeing assorted and deferential portrayal in games.

Inclusivity: creating games that are playable by all players and inclusive.

Staying away from Hurtful Practices: Avoiding plan decisions that might have adverse results.

Well-Being of Players Managing Play and Rest: Planning games that advance solid play propensities.

Tending to Habit Concerns: putting in place measures to reduce the risk of addiction.

Regarding Security: safeguarding player data and privacy in online games.

You'll learn all there is to know about the key elements that go into making games that are both engaging and enjoyable as you study game design principles. These standards will direct you in molding games that resound with players and stick to moral contemplations in the consistently advancing scene of game turn of events.

11. Troubleshooting and Advancement in Game Turn of events

11.1 Troubleshooting Strategies

Recognizing Bugs

Figuring out Normal Bugs: Perceiving normal issues like linguistic structure blunders, rationale mistakes, and runtime blunders.

Troubleshooting Devices: Investigating troubleshooting apparatuses and procedures accessible in coordinated advancement conditions (IDEs).

Logging: Executing logging to follow program stream and variable qualities during runtime.

Troubleshooting Methodologies

Breakpoints: Setting breakpoints to stop execution at explicit lines of code for examination.

Venturing Through Code: Utilizing bit by bit execution to dissect code conduct.

Watch and decide: Checking variable qualities continuously during investigating meetings.

11.2 Tools for Performance Optimization, Benchmarking, and Profiling:

Utilizing profiling apparatuses to break down code execution and distinguish bottlenecks.

Benchmarking: Leading execution benchmarks to gauge and think about various executions.

Advancement Measurements: Characterizing measurements to quantify the progress of advancement endeavors.

Code Improvement Procedures

Algorithmic Improvement: Working on the effectiveness of calculations for quicker execution.

Memory Enhancement: Overseeing memory use to diminish above and further develop execution.

Parallelization: Using equal handling for simultaneous execution of undertakings.

11.3 Illustrations and Delivering Streamlining

GPU Delivering

Figuring out GPU: Utilizing the force of Illustrations Handling Units (GPUs) for delivering.

Shader Enhancement: Creating effective shaders to improve the performance of graphics.

Clumping and Winnowing: Limiting the quantity of draw calls and delivering just apparent items.

Surface and Resource Advancement

Surface Pressure: Executing surface pressure for decreased memory use.

Level of Detail (LOD): Utilizing LOD procedures to change the degree of detail in light of distance.

Resource Stacking Systems: improving loading times by streamlining the loading of assets.

11.4 Reducing latency through network optimization

Understanding latency: locating the causes of latency in games played over a network.

Client Expectation: implementing prediction on the client side to lessen perceived lag.

Extending and Interpolating: Smoothing player development by introducing between network refreshes.

Data transmission Productivity

Information Pressure: Compacting network information for more proficient transmission.

Prioritization of Messages: Focusing on basic game occasions to improve data transmission utilization.

Limiting Update Recurrence: Sending just fundamental updates to decrease information move.

11.5 Cross-Stage Streamlining

Stage explicit Contemplations

Equipment Varieties: addressing the differences in performance between platforms and devices.

Input Dealing with: adjusting input handling for various devices and control schemes.

Goal and Viewpoint Proportion: Supporting different screen goals and viewpoint proportions.

Stage explicit APIs

Using Stage APIs: making use of platform-specific optimizations and features.

Improving for Portable: Carrying out versatile explicit improvements for execution and battery duration.

Console-explicit Improvements: Adjusting to the abilities and imperatives of gaming consoles.

11.6 Management of memory

Effective Memory Utilization Waste Collection: Understanding and dealing with the effect of trash assortment on execution.

Object Pooling: Reusing objects to reduce allocation and deal location of memory.

Memory Profiling: Examining memory utilization examples to distinguish regions for development.

Memory Leaks Memory Leak Detection: making use of tools to find and fix memory leaks

Reference Counting: Carrying out reference building up to oversee object lifetimes.

Tidying Up Assets: Appropriately delivering and overseeing assets to forestall memory spills.

11.7 Security and Code Improvement

Secure Coding Practices

Input Approval: Carrying out input approval to forestall security weaknesses.

Code Surveys: Directing code audits to recognize and address security gambles.

Authority and Authentication: ensuring that user authorization and authentication are handled securely.

Modular Design Modifiability of the Code: Coding in a modular and easy-to-maintain manner.

Documentation: Composing clear and extensive documentation for code clarity.

Version Management: Using variant control frameworks to follow changes and team up actually.

You will acquire the skills necessary to identify and resolve issues, improve performance, and guarantee the effective operation of your games across various platforms as you explore debugging and optimization in game development. These strategies are critical for conveying excellent gaming encounters to players.

12. Distributing Your Game

12.1 Getting ready for Delivery

Concluding Game Resources

Quality Affirmation: Directing intensive testing to recognize and determine any leftover issues.

Cleaning Illustrations and Sound: ensuring that each and every visual and auditory component possesses the desired quality.

Execution Streamlining: Calibrating the game for ideal execution on track stages.

Legitimate Contemplations

Protected innovation: ensuring that no game assets violate intellectual property rights and are properly licensed.

Security Approaches: Drafting and carrying out security strategies to conform to information assurance guidelines.

EULA (End-Client Permit Understanding): Making an unmistakable EULA to characterize how players can utilize the game.

12.2 Picking a Stage

Target Stages

PC/Macintosh/Linux: Choosing whether to deliver on work area stages and improving for various working frameworks.

Console Stages: Investigating potential chances to deliver on gaming control center and meeting stage necessities.

Platforms for Mobile: Taking into account iOS and Android stages for versatile game deliveries.

Online Stages and Stores

Steam, Legendary Games Store, and so on.: choosing digital distribution platforms for PC games after conducting research.

PlayStation Store, Xbox Store, and so on.: Understanding the accommodation cycle for console stages.

Google Play Store, Apple Application Store, and so forth.: navigating the app store requirements and guidelines.

12.3 Guidelines for submitting games

Platform-specific requirements: Complying with accommodation rules given by the picked stages.

Specialized Prerequisites: Meeting specialized determinations, including upheld goals and document designs.

Content Rules: Guaranteeing that game substance conforms to stage explicit substance strategies.

Confirmation and Testing

Quality Affirmation: Leading last testing to guarantee the game satisfies stage guidelines.

Certificate Cycle: submitting the game for console platform certification.

Beta Testing: Using beta testing to assemble criticism before the authority discharge.

12.4 Showcasing and Advancement

Making a Promoting Plan

Distinguishing Ideal interest group: Characterizing the segment for the game and fitting promoting methodologies appropriately.

Virtual Entertainment Presence: Utilizing virtual entertainment stages for advancement and local area commitment.

Press Unit: Making a complete press unit with limited time materials and data.

Trailers and Screen captures

Game Trailer: Creating a connecting with and useful game trailer to grandstand key elements.

Great Screen captures: Giving outwardly engaging screen

captures that catch the pith of the game.

Limited time Craftsmanship: creating artwork for use in promotional materials

12.5 Sending off Your Game

Delivery Date Determination

Timing Contemplations: Picking an ideal delivery date to amplify deceivability and effect.

Staying away from Contest: Staying away from swarmed discharge periods to limit contest.

Releases of Post-Launch Support Patches: Planning for present send off patches on address any issues found by players.

Local area Commitment: Remaining dynamic in the gaming local area, answering player criticism, and cultivating a positive local area.

Additional Information: Arranging and delivering extra satisfied, like updates, developments, or DLC.

12.6 Post-Send off Examination

Examination and Measurements

Player Measurements: Utilizing analytics tools to examine player engagement and behavior.

Deals and Income: Exploring deals information and income produced during the underlying send off.

Player Comments: Assembling and assessing input from players to illuminate future updates and undertakings.

Iterative Turn of events

Guide for Updates: Arranging a guide for post-send off updates and upgrades.

Iterative Plan: Utilizing post-send off examination to advise progressing advancement and refinement regarding the game.

Local area Contribution: Including the local area in decision-production for future updates.

Distributing your game is a critical achievement, and cautious preparation and execution are pivotal for progress. By following these means, you can explore the intricacies of the distributing system, boost the deceivability of your game, and construct a positive relationship with your player local area.

13. Extra Small Games

13.1 Small Game: Overview of the Memory Card Matching Game's Concept:

Matching game based on memory cards in which players flip cards to find pairs that match.

Objective: In the shortest amount of time and with the fewest moves, match all card pairs.

Execution

Card Framework: Make a network of face-down cards.

Game Rationale: Carry out rationale for flipping cards, checking for matches, and refreshing the game state.

Scoring: Keep track of how long it took to finish the game and how many moves it took.

Interface for Use: Create a user interface with card images and game statistics that looks good.

13.2 Smaller than expected Game:

Overview of the Whack-a-Mole Game Concept: Whack-a-Mole game where players endeavor to "whack" or tap on haphazardly seeming moles.

Objective: Hit however many moles as would be prudent inside a restricted time.

Mole Animation for Implementation: Make movable moles that appear and go away at random.

Scorekeeping: Track the player's score in light of fruitful hits.

Time Breaking point: Put in place a game's countdown timer.

Audio effects: Add drawing in audio cues for fruitful hits and misses.

13.3 Scaled down Game: Snake on a Matrix

Outline

Game Idea: An improved on form of the Snake game where the player controls a snake on a framework.

Objective: Develop the snake by eating food without crashing into the walls or itself.

Execution

Lattice Format: Create a game board with a grid.

Snake Development: Use user input to implement logic for the movement of the snake.

Food Age: Create food at irregular situations for the snake to eat.

Impact Location: Handle collisions with the snake's own body and walls.

Scoring Framework: Monitor the players score in light of the length of the snake.

13.4 Scaled down Game: Space Intruders

Outline

Game Idea: Exemplary space shooter where players control a spaceship to shield against sliding outsider trespassers.

Objective: Kill all outsider trespassers before they arrive at the lower part of the screen.

Execution

Player Spaceship: Make a controllable spaceship at the lower part of the screen.

Outsider Intruders: Create rows of descending, horizontally moving alien invaders.

Mechanism for Shooting: Give the player's spaceship a shooting mechanism.

Game Over Conditions: Characterize conditions for the game to end, for example, when outsiders arrive at the base or when the player's spaceship is hit.

13.5 Small Game: Puzzle Slider

Outline

Game Idea: Puzzle slider game where players improve rearranged pieces to reproduce a picture.

Objective: Rework the unique pieces to reproduce the first picture.

Execution

Picture Cutting: Sort an image into pieces for a puzzle.

Rearranging Instrument: The puzzle pieces should be shuffled at random for the player to solve.

Client Communication: Permit players to move parts of contiguous void openings.

Triumph Check: Decide when the riddle has been effectively addressed.

These extra smaller than expected games offer an assortment of ongoing interaction encounters and are magnificent for upgrading your game improvement abilities. Every scaled down game presents remarkable difficulties, like activity, scoring frameworks, and UIs, permitting you to additionally investigate various parts of game turn of events.

End

Congrats on finishing this complete Python Games Guide! All through this excursion, you've dove into different parts of game turn of events, beginning from the basics of programming in Python to cutting edge procedures and standards of game plan. Let's recap the most memorable aspects of your game development journey:

Python's foundations:

Gained a strong groundwork in Python programming.
Investigated essential ideas, for example, factors, information types, control stream, capabilities, and modules.
Prologue to Pygame:

Jumped into the universe of game advancement with Pygame.

learned how to handle user input, manage game states, and create basic games.

Exemplary Games Revamps:

Thought back about exemplary games by reproducing them in Python.

Carried out works of art like Pong, Breakout, and Space Trespassers to grasp game mechanics.

Animation and graphics:

Using Pygame, add animations and graphics to your games.

investigated drawing shapes, manipulating images, and putting dynamic animations into action.

Intuitive Narrating Games:

captivated players with text-based adventures and narratives based on choices with interactive storytelling.

GUI Games with Tkinter:

Extended your abilities by making graphical UI (GUI) games utilizing Tkinter.

Created games like Spasm Tac-Toe and Memory Puzzle with a visual connection point.

Games for Two Players:

Wandered into the domain of multiplayer game turn of events.

Found out about attachments, server-client engineering, and online multiplayer contemplations.

High level Game Advancement Procedures:

Investigated progressed ideas like physical science reenactments, computerized reasoning, expanded reality, and AI in games.

Game Plan Standards:

Dug into the standards of game plan, including player brain research, mechanics, UI/UX plan, narrating, and adaptation.

Troubleshooting and Streamlining:

Dominated procedures for troubleshooting code and streamlining game execution.

Distributing Your Game:

Investigated the method involved with planning, submitting, and showcasing your game for various stages.

Extra Smaller than expected Games:

Applied your abilities by making different small games, including memory card coordinating, Whack-a-Mole, Snake on a Network, Space Trespassers, and Puzzle Slider.

All in all, you've not just educated the specialized parts of game turn of events yet in addition acquired bits of knowledge into the imaginative and key parts of planning, testing, and delivering games. Recall that game improvement is a unique field, and consistent learning and trial and error are vital to remaining at the cutting edge of the business.

Whether you're leaving on a lifelong in game turn of events, chasing after private ventures, or just investigating your energy for making intelligent encounters, this guide has outfitted you with significant abilities and information. The universe of game advancement is immense and steadily advancing, so continue investigating, making, and pushing the limits of what you can accomplish with your freshly discovered aptitude in Python game turn of events.

I wish you a fun-filled and exciting future in the gaming industry! Blissful coding!